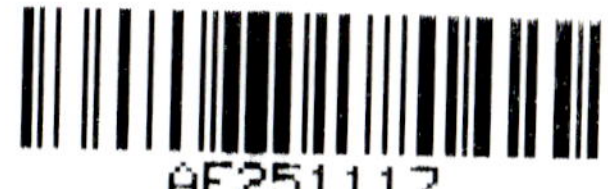

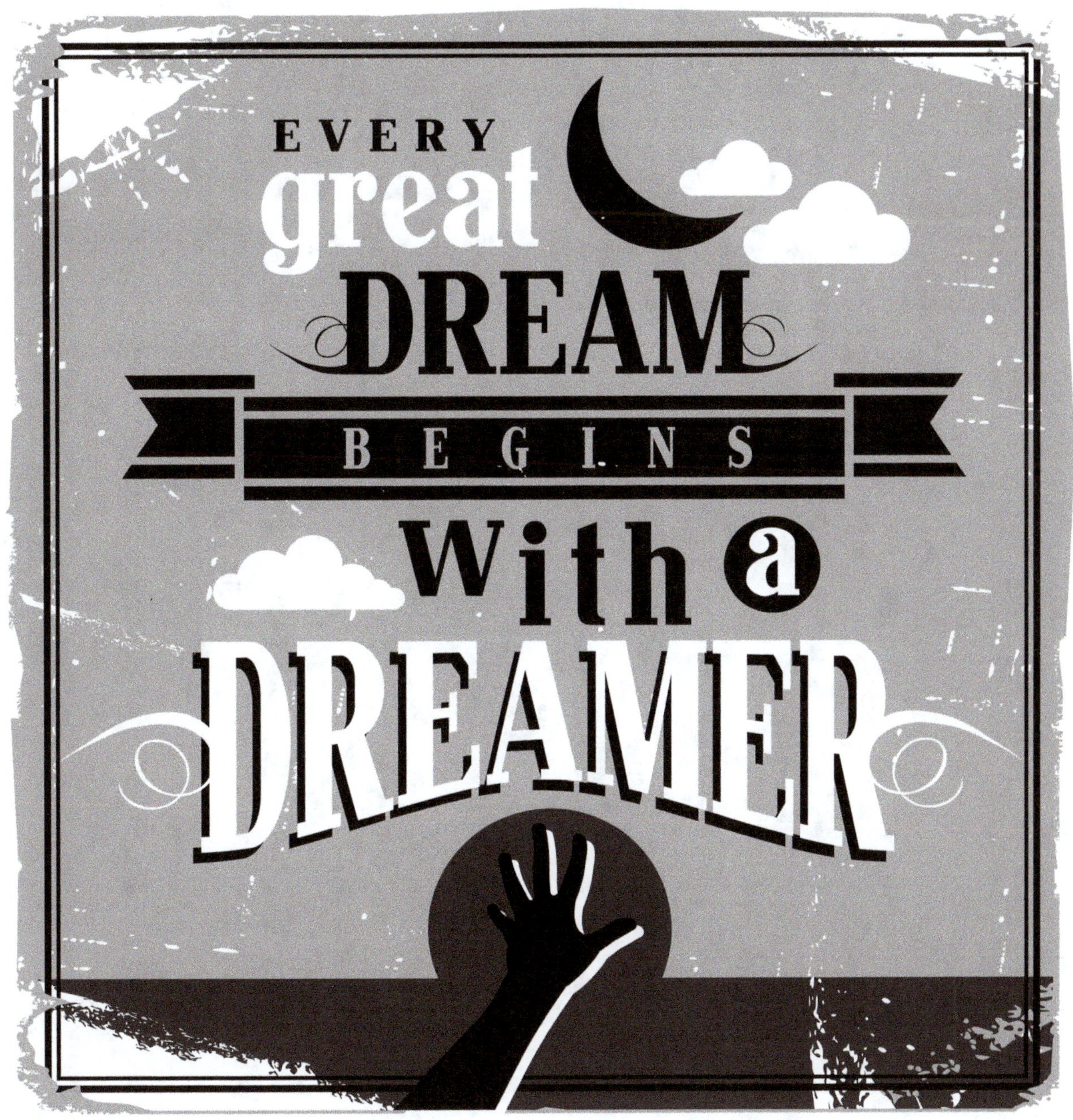

EVERY
great
DREAM
BEGINS
with a
DREAMER

THIS SKETCHBOOK BELONGS TO:

____

©2019 YOUNG DREAMERS PRESS